About the author

Andrew Brook was born in 1955 and is Bradford born and bred spending most of his life in the Heaton area. He attended St. Cuthbert's junior school and St Bede's grammar school.

On leaving school his first job was with Christopher Pratt's followed by a series of short scale positions before joining British rail as a freight guard, carrying amongst other things, nuclear warheads! He progressed to various clerical positions with British rail before taking voluntary redundancy. He then started a business of private investigators, which stood him in good stead for writing this book, sifting fact from fiction. He is currently working as an heir hunter tracing missing heirs and beneficiaries. Andrew stood as liberal candidate in the 1979 municipal elections for the Heaton district, obtaining a record vote which has never been beaten! He met his wife, Linda whilst back packing in Ghana, one of his nine trips to West Africa. The Author is related to crickets all time No 1, Wilfred Rhodes, from Kirkheaton, Huddersfield, and former undefeated WBA welterweight champion of world boxing, Ike Quartey of Ghana. Frank Warren refers to Ike as 'boxing's best kept secret' Andrew has a son, Marcus and enjoys walking and swimming amongst his pastimes. He can be found regularly walking over Ilkley Moor or Shipley Glen not just in exercising, but also taking in the breath taking views.

Andrew would like to thank Peter Gill for his help with this book and Idris Saadi for the idea to write it.

This book is dedicated to the memory of my late parents,
George and Irene

Preface

Bradford (Bradeford in 1086 and also called Broad Ford in history) is essentially a Victorian City whose fortunes have ebbed and flowed with the passage of time. Fortunes have been hewn from its sombre streets and history oozes up from every stone flag present, each with a tale to tell.

By the Edwardian era Bradford had inherited a provincial smugness and judging by the number of Rolls Royce's present looked down with a sense of disdain on its near neighbours in Leeds and Sheffield.

Trade had converted Bradford from a sleepy market town to "The most striking phenomena in the history of the British Empire". Bradford has a unique identity – its people being non-conformist in nature, a special resilience which has gone out to all four corners of the world. Today, even one the world's most former powerful men, had his roots in the city! Yes, old Dubya is a fifth generation Bradfordian by the name of George W Bush, Read on…….!

Copyright

No part of this publication may be reproduced, copied, edited or made available for public broadcast either digitally, in print or any other format without the publisher's written consent.

This notice extends to digitalised copy and reproduction

© Andrew Brook 2014

Contents

Chapter 1	In Ancient Times
Chapter 2	From the Norman Conquest
Chapter 3	In Transition 1200 – 1400
Chapter 4	The War of the Roses
Chapter 5	The Civil War
Chapter 6	Industrial Revolution and Worstedopolis
Chapter 7	Industrialisation
Chapter 8	Social Problems of Expansion
Chapter 9	The Jewish Merchants
Chapter 10	The Coming of the Railways
Chapter 11	Hospitals and Medicine
Chapter 12	The Two World Wars
Chapter 13	Fred Jowett
Chapter 14	Social Reform
Chapter 15	Undercliffe Cemetery
Chapter 16	The Italians in Bradford
Chapter 17	Irish Society in Bradford
Chapter 18	As Time Goes By
Chapter 19	Famous Bradfordians
Chapter 20	Past Lord Mayors of Bradford

Chapter 1

In Ancient Times

The name Bradford is derived from a ford or water crossing used before the Norman Conquest somewhere at the bottom of what is now known as Church Bank. The barbarians living in their mud huts would be unaware that in the future years Bradford would become one of the world's great manufacturing cities and "The greatest phenomenon in the history of the British Empire". The area, a city since 1897 is situated in a dome like cavity and built on seven hills situated close to a rich coal seam which was to become significant in Bradford's future industrial progression. Just outside the Bradford boundary in Hirst Wood some 2,000 years ago lived a prehistoric family one of the area's first farmers who lived in a stone and wood dwelling 53 feet in diameter. A further small holding in Buck Wood – an area of Thackley – the size of a football pitch featuring a raised platform and simple stone shelter could be dated back to Roman times. Let us start in AD 71 when the Romans occupied the north of England via Queen Cartimandua, leader of the Brigantian tribe of the Celts. Soon a series of roads would become evident, the most famous being the Roman highway from Ilkley (just outside Bradford) to Manchester. This highway takes the route of Toller lane to it's junction with Haworth road and Bingley road, along to Stoney Ridge and on to Lee Lane at Cottingley. It continues to Harden Moor and on to Elslack near Skipton. There was probably a Roman road traversing eastwards from Ribchester in the Ribble Valley through the Aire Valley and touching upon various areas which were to become suburbs of Bradford and leading on to Pontefract. Roman coins have been found in the Heaton area and, although without foundation, it has been said 5,000 men of Emperor

Hadrian's 9th legion (of Spanish descent) were massacred in the Crossflats area. They were paid in silver coins. In 1775 a chest was discovered containing 30,000 silver coins at Morton Banks near Bingley, together with a silver figure of Goddess Cybele. Many carved heads; usually about a foot high were produced by the Brigantes. Sidney Jackson, former curator at Cartwright hall in the 1960's took a special interest in these stone products. Two schoolgirls found Celtic stone heads in a dry wall in the Heaton suburb of Bradford. The Romans brought great culture and engaged in the manufacturing of iron. Eventually they returned home to defend their homelands in around 410 AD, leaving Britain, as well as Bradford undefended. This left an opportunity for war like Picts and Scots to invade the area and in turn the Anglos and their relatives, the Friesians found a place to call home! The seventh century became known as the 'Dark Ages'. There is not much known about this period only the possibility of great weather change. The Saxons or 'Southern Danes' were the next race to show their faces in the area. After having conquered York and the Dales they divided the area that was to become Yorkshire into 'the ridings', or what was commonly to become known as 'Ridings' until 1974 when they were officially abolished under local government re-organisation after almost a thousand years. Even today, certain areas of Bradford still reflect their Danish origins and inhabitants. One particular example, being the south Bradford suburb of Wyke, a farmstead or wick other areas of Bradford including Manningham are shown to be early Saxon settlements. So for the first thousand years, and Bradford's ever changing face, the next hundred years were to bring profound changes, probably for the better, from our new colonizers.

Chapter 2

From the Norman Conquest onwards

Just after 1000 AD England for the first time was relatively united considering the number of invasions it had endured on its shores during the last thousand years.

Bradfordale, that it had become, had around 350 inhabitants living in single dwelling farms or small agricultural communities. A single Anglo Saxon man called Gamel ruled the area. The Norman Invasion of 1066 totally transformed the lives of Bradfordale residents...

The area was laid to waste after a rebellion by the locals in the north of England and many of its occupants put to the sword. The Manor of Bradfordale was given a four pound valuation for taxation purposes to its Norman landlord. Ilbert De Lacey and Bradfordale residents become slaves to the agricultural system of the time.

Large numbers of Normans with their families came to settle in the area, even though the area remained profitless for its landlords. If the Norman invasion was not enough for the Bradfordale residents, more misery would be heaped upon them.

The Scottish people sent down raiding parties, they gained access through Skipton! They took away large numbers of people from the area so that every small dwelling in the southern part of Scotland had its own English slave.

Chapter 3

In Transition 1200 – 1400

Ilbert de Lacy now fully controlled the manor of Bradfordale, taking over from Anglo Saxon tribal chieftain Gamel. The De Lacy's were to rule over Bradfordale for almost the next 250 years and still standing today is a public house on Tong street, The De Lacy, named after this famous family. Such was the Norman the Conqueror's concern about his unruly northern subjects that a series of castles were built at various points across Yorkshire. The major one being built in Pontefract in 1070 and then Ilbert de lacy was to become Baron of Pontefract. It is believed a castle existed at some time in Bradford. To my knowledge, the first church became evident in 1281 and records show that the parish received a legacy of 96 acres of land from the Delacy's, who were seen to be a devout religious family. The church of Bradfordale had to pay its mother church in Dewsbury the sum of eight shillings per year, but for what?

Bradfordale's population was now growing and facilitated a market. In 1251 the manor's first market resided in the vicinity of the parish church (now the Cathedral) and later moving on to the bottom of Westgate and where still stands a market cross residing in the entrance to the Arndale shopping centre. The population of Bradfordale existed along a line from present day Barkerend North West through Kirkgate and Westgate, past the market areas and along to what is now White Abbey road.

The male heirs of the De Lacy's now became extinct and the manor of Bradfordale passed to the Earls of Lancaster and their Duchy's.

The De Lacy's had carried out their duties empowered to them by the

Duke of Lancaster to collect taxes, keep the peace and provide recruits for war. For a short period of time the manor of Bradfordale passed to Philippa, the black queen, wife of Edward III who received the area by a strange twist of fate as her husband was considered a spendthrift by his mother, no dowry was granted and because of this the 'Manor' of Bradfordale and the title 'The Honour of Pontefract' was granted.

The next incumbent of these titles was John of Gaunt, the fourth son of Edward III who was in effect the Kings Vassal together with his Spanish wife Eleanor. Apparently John rode through the streets of Bradford in shining armour and full regalia 'to a rude people' who were loyal to their lords, this was pure feudalism. John's entourage walked down Church Bank to the market cross at Westgate and up Whetley Hill and on to Lancashire.

It seems certain at this time the manor of Bradford consisted of a great deal of woodland above and beyond the present day cathedral and in an area called Cliffe Woods, which today would be the triangle of Valley road, Canal road and Bolton road. In this area a wild boar was known to exist. It roamed freely and caused great nuisance! So much so, that a reward was offered by the authority to kill the beast. A local young man took on the beast with his sword and managed to kill it. Quickly he cut off the boars tongue and placed it in his pocket and raced to the local market in Kirkgate to claim his reward of a purse full of gold, land at Great Horton and the job of watchman.

His name is not clear, but could possibly be Roger de Manningham who was seen to occupy the hunt yard at Great Horton. Even today the boars head is still evident in the Bradford coat of arms. Probably the most important document since the Doomsday book was now about to be produced- an inquisition of all lands belonging to Henry de Lacy of Lincoln at his death in 1310 at the age of 60.

The township of Bradford covered about 1600 acres and roughly 100 families living in the area. These calculations based on agricultural acreage. Records produced in Latin show the total wealth of the Earl of Lincoln to be about forty pounds for his Bradford area yet he did not control all of the manors in the vicinity and his tenants consisted of five separate classes. Unfortunately plague was to affect the area over the next sixty or seventy years and consequently the economic fortunes of Bradford were to take a downturn.

The next phase in Bradford's history was the changeover from agricultural production to small scale domestic woollen production driven by the fact of partial inheritance of property and land making it uneconomic for the working population to continue in their old objectives. The name Frizinghall is possibly derived from the Flemish word 'frieze' which is a type of cloth and showed that some small scale type of textile production was taking place in the area at that time.

Upon the death of John of Gaunt in 1399 the duchy of Lancaster including the manor of Bradford, passed to his son Henry de Bollingbroke, who at the time of his father's death was in exile, which gave King Richard ll chance to seize such lands. Unfortunately for King Richard they did not belong to him for long as a couple of months later Henry de Bollingbroke returned from exile and dethroned the king. Bradford therefore belonged to the crown and we entered into an unstable era of almost forty years racked by the war between the houses of York and Lancaster with some of the bloodiest battles being fought locally and with men from the Bradford area.

City of Bradford Coat of Arms

Chapter 4

The Wars of the Roses

Being in the Yorkshire region Bradford should have supported the white rose. But by a strange twist of fate and coupled with the fact that Bradford at that time was governed by the Duchy of Lancaster, its inhabitants took the side of the red rose. The powerful Clifford family of Skipton were fervently on the side of the Lancastrians and this could have swayed the side of the Bradford people. A local prominent landowner, Robert Bolling, occupied what is now Bolling Hall Museum, and was a supporter of both the Clifford family and the Lancastrians who were defeated at the battle of Towton Moor near York on Psalm Sunday 1461. The local beck ran red for several days such was the severity of the battle. The Yorkists, having won a decisive victory at Towton duly appointed Edward, the son of the Duke of York, to be crowned at Westminster. Many Local landowners duly lost their land including Robert Bolling, who petitioned against such action and was granted a pardon. This was surprising as it was the first occasion he had fought against the crown. After the War of the Roses had finished Bradford was about to enter a period of relative stability, the first occasion this had happened for over four hundred years. The city began to prosper and feudalism was almost dead. The crown was being replaced by local gentry such as the Bollings and the Tempests who took the opportunity to raise rents by large amounts and with their tenants naturally objecting to the large increases. The main courts which existed at the top of Ivegate were in frequent use and this was where compromises were often reached. Bradford's population was increasing along with trade due to the stability of the Tudor monarchs. Population at that time was in the region of 2,000 souls and the town was acquiring a reputation as a place of shoemakers and at least two dozen clothiers.

The present parish church had also been completed. Henry VIII was now King and the owner of the Duchy of Lancaster. Henry was not reaping the benefit of this increase in trade and passed the stewardship of Bradford to a William Rawson for a small sum. Rawson became clerk of the court of Bradford and took every opportunity to oppress his local tenants. He lived in a considerable pile called Bradford Hall for his trouble. After some years of prosperity, Bradford again hit a crisis. The new monarch Henry VIII was unable to hold more than one wife simultaneously according to the Church of Rome. He broke away from the said Church, formed his own Church of England and destroyed a local monastery and also a nunnery at Esholt. Bradford therefore escaped relatively lightly! The local land gentry, being mostly Catholic naturally went against their kings actions and formed the pilgrimage of Grace (1536). Local squire Sir Richard Tempest of Bolling Hall died for his actions but others lower down the social scale did benefit. Monastic lands were sold off and broader ownership became apparent. The Bradford people generally accepted the reformation of the Church, hence the growth of Puritanism and the textile trade.

Towton Cross

Towton Moor Memorial, This site witnessed one of the bloodiest battles in English history, yet very much forgotten.

Chapter 5

The Civil War

The monarch at the time, Charles I, believed in the divine right of Kings, his parliament thought otherwise hence the division between the two. Charles almost 20 years earlier finding his father James I, was heavily in debt to the city of London and had to sell the manor of Bradford. The population of Bradford were dissatisfied with their King and became alienated from him due to the tithing system of taxation. The 6,000 inhabitants were further incensed of a new papist vicar to the manor, Richard Hudson.

Open war was declared between King and Parliament. King Charles, feeling not safe in London had removed his court to York. Proceedings for battle locally began in earnest on Sunday December 18th 1642 at about 10am when the locals were attending church, at which now is the Cathedral. The Royalist representing the crown proceeded to attack the Cathedral but they were dispersed by the Parliamentarian's amateur soldiers.

The Royalists were eventually forced back, into the Barkerend area, this was known locally as the 'battle of the steeple' or the first siege of Bradford. The battle lasted eight hours. News travelled round the country and raised the awareness of the Parliamentary cause. The Royalists labelled the Parliamentarians the 'popish' army and for the time being had been defeated. The Earl of Newcastle was in control of other towns in West Yorkshire and tried to impose an economic blockade on Bradford. A further battle was fought at Adwalton Moor, near Driglington some six miles from Bradford in the summer of 1643 between Lord Fairfax, representing the Parliamentarians and the Earl of Newcastle for the Royalists. This proved to be a decisive victory for the latter. Lord Fairfax retreated to Hull leaving Bradford open to siege for the second time. The Earl of Newcastle then proceeded to surround the town of Bradford and made his headquarters at Bolling Hall on a hill above the town. The local inhabitants were terrified. The Parliamentarians enclosed themselves in the Cathedral whilst the church steeple was heavily laden with wool sacks which were quickly shot down. Lord Fairfax, knowing he was hopelessly defeated fled to Leeds via Barkerend Road, but his wife was captured at the point where paper hall stands.

The Earl of Newcastle had given orders that every man, woman and child be killed. These orders were given days before the siege but a ghost appeared whilst the Earl slept on the night before the battle and stated 'Pity poor Bradford'. This had a profound effect on the Earl who changed his orders therefore sparing many of the Bradfordians lives. Instead the town was plundered by the royalist soldiers who took away whatever they could. Bradford had paid a heavy price and played no further part in the civil war. The town was to further suffer for more than a hundred years with the destruction of its wool trade due to the bubonic plague and its opposition to the monarchy.

Bolling Hall had changed hands many times from the point of the civil war, but even today remains the most haunted house in the Bradford district with many sightings and still continuing in recent times. The bubonic plague it is thought was brought to Bradford in a bundle of clothes. Many residents who were considered infected were taken to a place called Cliff Barn in Undercliffe and food brought to a spot some way away from the barn. The dead were buried in local woodland. Leading

Bradfordians at the time further conspired against the King making Bradford's chances of economic recovery remote in the short term. Many Parliamentarians suffered fines or were sent to jail. Therefore, for the last six hundred years, Bradford's prosperity had ebbed and flown to reach great heights only to be brought down to earth with a bang. Communication and transport were to prove positive in the not too distant future.

Chapter 6

The Industrial Revolution and the rise of Worstedopolis

Bradford and England had been an agricultural country and the area was now undergoing a radical change. Instead of exporting corn and other products worked by hand labour, machines began to appear worked by mechanical power, the first power being water, particularly in the West Riding.

Coal and iron were now important, so too were cotton and wool. Men and women were working in factories for an hourly wage rate. New roads and canals had to be provided for transport of materials, particularly coal. The power loom of 1785 was invented by Cartwright (the current Cartwright Hall in Bradford being named after him) this piece of machinery was powered by water and introduced in Bradford in 1826 after the wool comber's strike of 1825. A few mills were present in the area at the time, the first being in 1798 at what is now called Quebec Street and naturally the wool used was of Bradford descent. The fast expanding industry now began to use steam engines with copious amounts of coal being available locally and cheaply. Bradford's future motto on its coat of arms 'LABOR OMNI VINCIT' translated states 'work conquers all' and was proving very apt. After the wool combers strike of 1825 life was still very hard for the man in the street although the city was still continuing to prosper.

Due to its increase in manufactured trade England was able to defeat Napoleon. Due to this defeat and heavy taxation to finance such, other European countries were unable to purchase English goods. Many people locally lost their jobs and had to apply to the local poor law authorities for assistance. Large numbers of workers were idle and work creation schemes were introduced. The main scheme in Bradford being the clearing out of Bradford beck and wages were set at one shilling a day. Bradford had now overtaken Halifax as the main centre of production for worsteds due to being in a superior graphical location. The Leeds/Liverpool canal was built in 1770 but not completed until 1816. Heavy goods were known to be sent cheaper by water than by road. Locally many of the roads were called 'turnpike' roads whereby taxes were levied, hence Toller lane. The poor people resented these roads fearing they were subsidising the rich and attendant commerce. A piece hall was opened in 1773 built in what is now Piccadilly. Mr John Hustler, a local manufacturer was the main financier for the hall and Hustlergate in Bradford is named after him. The same gentleman was one of the main promoters for the Leeds/Liverpool canal. All the foundations were now in place for Bradford to move forward in the race for industrialisation. In the space of twenty years mills in Bradford had increased from five to thirty one. Worstedopolis was now firmly upon us!

Census returns for Bradford in 1801 show the population to be 13,246 with the number of people working in the worsted manufacturing business to be 1,290. Over the next 50 years the population grew to 104,000. 200 factories now existed and Frederick Engels in his book 'The Condition of the Working Class of England' stated Bradford to be one of the filthiest towns he had ever visited. Many workers went about barefoot particularly women and children. Nine year old children worked roughly six hours a day, while thirteen year olds worked longer. Industrial work was seen by Engels to be the greatest social evil. One of the alternatives to factory work and unemployment was the workhouse brought about by the poor law of 1834. The only relief offered to the poor was free admission to certain establishments. The food available was of poor quality and in return the pauper had to work even harder than in a normal job. The person who failed to work generally went without food. Fathers, mothers and children were housed in separate sections of the workhouse and only allowed to see each other on rare fixed intervals. All this contributed to bad health. Factory chimneys poured out black sulphurous smoke and sewage was dumped in the Bradford beck.

There were regular outbreaks of cholera and typhoid. Only 30% of children born to textile workers in the area lived to reach the age of 15. People could not afford the attention of a doctor so the labouring population resorted to cheaper remedies, sometimes having disastrous consequences. Drink, as ever were the curse of the working class and the temptation of drinking in excess led many to the rocky road of ruin. Many workers lay helpless in the gutter after visiting beer houses and gin palaces.

A new governing body was established by an act of Parliament to deal with light, cleansing and paving. Twenty two mutual friendly societies were said to exist in Bradford in the early 1800's with 2,500 members although Bradford had few thoroughfares at that time with only Westgate, kirkgate, Tyrrel Street, Market Street and Bridge street. Sunday schools had been introduced to teach children to read and write while their daily toll between Monday and Sunday continued unaffected. The first savings bank opened in 1818, The East Morley and Bradford Savings Bank, although fifteen years earlier the Quaker Harris family had formed Peckover, Harris and Co to the old Bradford bank in Kirkgate. The Harris family showed their true colours and formed many charities in the Bradford area. A Roman Catholic Church was built on East Parade in 1825, previous to this Catholics who wished to worship had to walk to Leeds to do so.

Two local newspapers started within days of each other. Firstly The Bradford Courier and West Riding Advertiser quickly followed by The Bradford and Wakefield Chronicle, Bradford was now in flux, a battle between capital and labour. The first power looms were set up in 1826 and combers and weavers wages dropped as a consequence. Men and women had come from the countryside to Bradford's new found wealth, but because of the power loom advances now suffered. The speed at which the town had grown in terms of population also created problems with sanitation. In 1803 a special panel of 58 commissioners were appointed to basically protect the health and safety of all locals, trying to control a population escalating out of control was very difficult as more people moved into the Bradford area and further more people built houses on land they owned close to the Bradford beck. Sometimes heavy rain together with the by-products of the textile industry would overflow the beck and create attendant problems. Health began to suffer and the death rate increased and rates had to be levied on properties which were inhabited during the 1830's and they increased on a regular scale up to about two shillings in the pound in 1840. With so many committees appointed to control the wellbeing of local's problems arose as to the defining boundaries of responsibility, due to these problems a town council had to be planned including a democratic election which was not evident with the commissioners. At the initial public meeting a majority were against applying for a charter of incorporation and a certain minority of the population took the matter further and canvassed the area enabling signatures to be obtained to petition Queen Victoria for a charter. While 8,700 ratepayers were in favour of a charter there were 10,500 against. The pro charter party did not give up and made it known to Bradfordians how important and necessary the charter would be in the future of their town. In 1846 the charter party sent another party petition to the Queen and in 1847 a charter of incorporation was granted enabling a mayor, fourteen aldermen (elected by councillors) and forty two councillors presided over the municipality of eight wards. They were responsible for lighting and cleaning the streets and had control over the police force, thought to be less than one dozen officers (which was why the military had to be called for occasionally) A Scotsman, Mr Robert Milligan was elected Mayor. 80 worsted mills, 16 dye works, 8 corn mills, 250 warehouses, 40 collieries and some 22 stone quarries existed. It must be noted that a councillor had to have £1,000 of property or to be rated at least thirty pounds a year to be elected. Only 5.457 of Bradford's then population of 66,718 had sufficient qualification to be elected.

Chapter 7

Industrialisation

"The most striking phenomena in the history of the British Empire", These words describe Bradford's rise from a sleepy market town in the early 1800's to a dynamic and prosperous textile town by the early 1850's.

From a population of 13,000 in 1801 the population of Bradford had swollen to over 103,000 in 1851. More than half of these being immigrants, many from Ireland escaping the potato famine and a large number coming in from the countryside looking for work as the new reforms poor law which basically stated that those who come prepared for work can find it. A workhouse test was established in 1834 forcing the workshy to obtain employment or to use other charities and friends for support. 'The tough love workhouses' forced Charles Dickens to mention workers of being gradually starved in the workhouses. So Bradford enjoyed a plentiful supply of cheap labour. In 1843 the Bradford Observer newspaper had noted that the town was infested with thieves and vagabonds whom of which many might have turned to because of the workhouse test of 1834. Riot, drunkenness and street fighting were commonplace together with highway robbery.

The number of people working in the worsted industry in 1850 was listed at 33,515. Bradford was now the fastest rising population in England. 129 spinning mills now existed and as such, mills used thirteen times more wool as in 1810. The number of persons employed was more than half of the total textile workforce in all of Yorkshire. The textile factories produced copious amounts of smoke and only 30 per cent of children born to textile workers lived to reach the age of 15 and the general life expectancy in Bradford was 18 years.

Titus Salt, a prominent local businessman sought to remedy the situation. He had noted that the 'Rodda Smoke Burner' seemed to produce little pollution and placed them in his various business premises but had no luck in persuading other mill owners to do the same. On becoming the Mayor of Bradford in 1848 he used the opportunity to persuade the council to pass a by law making these burners compulsory – but failed. This was one of the main reasons he decided to make a model village in Saltaire. This model village was out of town and in 1852 Titus began the building, provision was for 4,500 workers. Educational needs for the workers were provided and medical needs were met by the enlightened textile owner. He also provided houses in his village for his workers. Generally the workers had a level of welfare not seen before, and a contented workforce it assumed would naturally give higher returns of Alpaca and Mohair goods. Many of the other textile workers in the area were not so fortunate. Fortunes in wealth continued to be made and lost in the textile trade and sometimes made again. With hard work and good fortune it was the 'sky's the limit' for some mill owners and such owners were looked upon as kings by their workforce. At the time the message went out that if you want to become a millionaire businessman come to Bradford!

The 'Half time' scheme gives the mill owners an unlimited supply of cheap labour. Once a week a child would start work at say 6am working till noon, then have his meal and go to school in the afternoon. The next week the situation would be reversed, school in the morning and mill work in the afternoon.

Chapter 8

Social Problems of Expansion

Bradford was destined to become the world's metropolis for wool – but there were social problems now evident. The huge influx of workers and many young children required some form of education. A government inspector in 1830 referred to Bradford as the dirtiest, filthiest and worst regulated town in the Kingdom.

The new merchant class became aware of their responsibilities and schools of many kinds soon appeared; night schools, ragged schools, Sunday schools and charity schools. Ragged schools saved children from drunkenness and crime and to provide a basic education in writing, reading and arithmetic and were the forerunners of the 1870 Education Act of the Bradford MP W.E.Forster.

In 1833 the government started to make annual grants of £20,000 per annum for elementary education and the grant was further increased to £40,000 per annum. Roughly 4,000 pupils attended various schools supervised by 700 teachers. These were the first signs of progression towards a common school system. In 1841 a school for factory children was started, three years after the first Manningham Mills was built by Mr S C Lister (afterwards Lord Masham).

Dr Scoresby was the Vicar of Bradford for seven years 1839 to 1846. He found that no child received daily education during the week from the local parish church. He attempted to give the town parochial schools and travelled the country preaching, to return with collections and donations.

This in turn produced ten schools but in the end Bradford children's education was beyond the work of one man. In 1850 a ragged school was started In Thornton Road and a further one in 1854 on Cropper Lane but the major factor in continuing education was W. E. Forster born in Bradpole, Dorset in 1818. His first occupation being wool sorting which he called 'dirty drudgery'. He later joined T S Fison as wool staplers and despite this found time to become chairman of the board of guardians and felt he should attempt to enter parliament to further reform the social conditions that so appalled him. In 1861 he was returned to parliament unopposed as a liberal MP.

The Bradford Population took him to their hearts and he was returned to office on no less than 6 occasions. His most famous conquest was the Education Act of 1870. This was an Act for common universal education and allowing for the election of the Bradford School Board. Religious, factory and private schools were in evidence at the time attempting to give 19,000 children, out of a total of roughly 80,000 children, a good start in life. The Bradford residents were happy with the passing of the act because it was neutral with no conditions attached and no allegiance to religion or business. The school boards were the forerunners of the state education system as we know it today.

In 1890 a vast crowd turned out to pay tribute to Forster and a statue was unveiled in his honour. Four years earlier his funeral had taken place in Westminster Abbey. Bradford was now providing work, education, hope and prospects for its population and continued to lead Britain in the field of social provision for its workers.

Chapter 9

The Jewish Merchants

The great increase in trade was brought about mainly by Germanic – Jewish merchants. In 1827 there were no foreign worsted merchants but a trickle became a flood after a German - Jewish trader named Jacob Behrens came to Bradford via Leeds to establish an export business of textiles. By 1847 there were 34 Germanic – Jewish merchants operating in the town, and a special business quarter off Leeds road became known as 'Little Germany'. These people of Jewish decent bestowed upon Bradford a huge cultural legacy. A certain doctor Bronner, a refugee, established the Bradford Eye and ear hospital and Jacob Behrens together with Jacob Arnold Unna founded the Bradford Chamber of Commerce in 1851. One of its first jobs was to create a code of practice including by laws for the settlement of disputes by arbitration. Leo Schuster was the first immigrant in Bradford to build premises. He paid 25 shillings a yard for land; he was also one of the first settlers of Jewish descent into Bradford. Other notable Jews that were born in Bradford were Delius, Rothenstein and Jonathan Silver, all of who will be mentioned in more detail later in this book.

The first Jewish synagogue was opened in Bowland Street off Manningham Lane. A second synagogue was opened in 1906 at Spring Gardens. These adherents to the faith were mainly of the reform persuasion. In 1875 a Bradford branch of the Anglo-Jewish Association was formed. The local businessmen threw themselves into charity work and consequently two Bradford Lord Mayors were of Germanic decent. The famous Bradford writer J B Priestley stated 'They were so much a part of the place when I was a boy' and 'I saw their outlandish names on office doors'. Even the Priestly birthplace at Mannheim Road off Toller Lane left its mark on the city together with neighbouring Bonn and Heildberg Road. Apart from these street names today little is left of the legacy of these people who catapulted Bradford to prominence in the textile trade. The importance of these men cannot be stressed highly enough, they did not merely bring trade, but also a culture all of their own.

The Behrens family mausoleum in Undercliffe Cemetery shows the prominence and standing of the family.

Chapter 10

The Coming of the Railways

By the mid 1840's, most major towns and cities had a railway system, but not Bradford.

For fifteen years Bradford tried to make a connection. In 1845 the scheme for a through railway line succeeded with the first line open from Leeds via Shipley. In 1846 the Leeds and Bradford line was extended to Keighley by a branch line from Shipley. Royal assent was given to a bill for railway communication with Low Moor, Halifax, Cleckheaton and Brighouse. The railway builders were presented with a great challenge due to Bradford's unusual geography which was to prove fatal at a later stage in Bradford's development.

After the initial lines had been constructed the engineers were kept busy for another 40 years giving Bradford further connections to Lancashire, London, the north and Scotland. By the mid 1850's Bradford consisted of three main stations. Bradford exchange with 10 platforms was regarded as off putting. What proved to be the problem of Bradford's railways was the non-connection of the north and south sections which was talked about for a great deal of time, but bore no fruit apart from a Shipley to Laisterdyke line via Idle for freight until 1964.

In the 1950's Bradford was accommodated by six express passenger trains including the 'Yorkshire Pullman' and the 'Devonian' to Paignton in Devon, these lasted until the 1960's. Forster Square became a parcels centre late in the 1960's with seventy porters based here, mainly African Asians who had fled Uganda and the Amin regime. The exchange station on Drake Street closed in the early 1970's to be replaced by a four platform station called the Interchange which had an adjoining bus station.

It is sad to see the demise of local railway links including the huge freight yards that once existed for the transport of textiles. This is especially so as the author is an ex railwayman and having worked at most of the local sites including the motive power department at Bowling Back Lane which closed in 1984.

Bradford's decline as an industrial centre can be reflected in its lack of current day railway connections and the lack of foresight by failing to connect the two stations, Exchange and Forster Square to make a through line.

Chapter 11

Hospitals and Medicine

Bradford at the beginning of the nineteenth century had a reputation for poor sanitation and childbirth threatened the lives of local mothers including the Reverend Patrick Bronte's wife whose many children died through scarlet fever. Overcrowding in many small houses and lack of proper water supply and sanitation contributed heavily to the problem. Prior to 1834 the Poor Law did give relief to the sick and destitute by way of payment of doctor's bills. The first Bradford dispensary opened in 1825 with Dr John Simpson in attendance along with surgeon John Blakey. By the end of its first year in operation almost 2,500 patients had been seen. In 1827 a new dispensing building was opened in Darley Street at a cost of £3,500 pounds. Gradually the number of patients began to rise and one dozen beds were provided by 1834.

In 1843 the first part of the infirmary and dispensary in Westgate was opened and the Independent Order of Oddfellows raised 600 guineas for such building. In 1848 a surveyor had reported locally that 'masses of filth in all directions were giving off foul stenches'. A cholera epidemic followed and deaths numbered 424. This problem not only showed itself in Bradford but throughout the urban centres of the north of England. Extra porters had to be employed to bury the victims. In the following years chloroform became available as an anaesthetic. The nursing staff at the time consisted of four untrained women who on many occasions were carried out to a bed themselves in a state of drunkenness. Attending for treatment at the time must have been a frightening experience for the patients. The infirmary was supplemented by the workhouse infirmary for over sixty years but the inmates suffered terrible conditions at Little Horton. Care was sometimes carried out by lunatics who were illiterate and therefore unable to carry out proper duties and correct prescriptions. In 1852 Doctor Bronner began five years of work for the poor persons suffering ear and eye problems which in turn led to the founding of the hospital of such name in 1857 to be followed by enlargement of the infirmary with a third storey in 1864 and a dispensary building added in 1869, and the first appointment of a medical officer of health in 1873. 11 years later it was decided a new wing should be created for the infirmary at the Lumb Lane end. Nearly all medical men in the town signed a petition against work in the evenings for under 10's.

A children's hospital was established in 1883 which was entirely voluntary and based on public subscription. Hanover Square was its headquarters. After four years it removed to Springfield Place in the former Springfield school. 1889 saw a further move to a one acre plot on Saint Mary's road, Manningham where there were two large wards, two smaller ones, an admin block and an isolation ward for infected cases. Four years later sight and hearing tests became evident in Bradford schools. The infirmary was allowed to add "Royal" in 1897 and in 1910 a new site was acquired at field house. During 1914 the local corporation agreed to purchase the new buildings at a consideration of £100,000 providing certain conditions were met. The following year the city of Bradford maternity hospital opened with an electric incubator. This was the first municipal ante natal clinic in England to be followed in 1929 by a system of annual group contributions for the maintenance of St Lukes hospital by trade unions and friendly societies. Some 46 contributory societies with 10,200 members benefited here. Opening a nursery school in Bradford the owner declared "Bradford is the Mecca of reform in all that concerns physical and technical education"

Chapter 12

The Two World Wars

With the advent of war everybody pulled together in the face of adversity. A conscript of some standing to be in the future literary world, was one J B Priestley, men and boys joined up and their regiment becoming known as the 16th Battalion prince of Wales own West Yorkshire regiment. A second Battalion the 18th became known as the Bradford Pals. From the 16th Battalion two thirds were killed in combat in the bloody battle known as the Battle of the Somme. Yes, Bradford knew what it was to be at war, what a waste of young lives! Bradford was numbed as the news filtered through.

During the First World War there was a disaster on Bradford's own doorstep at the Low Moor Munitions Company on August 21st 1916. A fire started and spread to lead to a series of explosions over two days. 339 people were killed, 60 were injured and two thousand local homes were destroyed or damaged.

The Second World War was different, old Bradford was in the firing line this time. Five air attacks hit Bradford, but probably the worst was on the night of August 31st 1940. It was reported that over one hundred people were injured, one killed and 60 families left homeless. Lingards department store was destroyed. Bradford was wide open to attack but had no defence mechanisms in place. Food rationing became commonplace and became the chief topic of conversation for many. Self-sufficiency became the norm and the black market flourished. Rationing continued until 1953. Air raid shelters also became evident with the dreaded warning sirens the nightmare facing all Bradfordians.

Remarkably, Bradford got off lightly in comparison with other industrial cities and a war memorial was erected after the First World War in 1922 by the Alhambra theatre made of local stone. Blueprints were drawn up to redesign Bradford after the Second World War.

The old architecture had stood up well to the bombing. People were becoming ashamed of the black sooted buildings which had served its textile industry so well for over one hundred years. In the early 1950's Stanley Wardley became chief engineer and surveyor and his ambition was to make Bradford a city of the future. Systematically he demolished Swan Arcade, Kirkgate Market and the Mechanics Institute, all wonderful buildings. Swan Arcade was replaced by Arndale House designed by a certain John Poulson.

The replacements that took place of the old buildings were cheap monstrosities that had no merit. J B Priestley was one of the biggest critics of the destruction of the wonderful old buildings.

Chapter 13

Fred Jowett and the legacy he left Bradford

By 1882 Bradford's population expansion had slowed down and only continued to grow as its boundaries grew to accumulate other suburbs now being included in its area. The upwardly mobile population retreated from the heartland of industrial Bradford to the more affluent suburbs of Heaton and Allerton. Until after that First World War Bradford was considered as the most progressive place in the UK. Culture was still evident and enriched by choral societies, music halls and theatres along with three daily newspapers and better known people than any other comparable sized city in the UK.

A man who kept Bradford in the limelight was one Frederick William Jowett who won a seat on the city council in November 1892 as the first socialist councillor to win a seat in a contested election. He worked vigorously on behalf of all of his constituents, particularly the unemployed. He pulled 1201 votes and was carried on the shoulders of his supporters after his victory. As yet there was no independent labour party (ILP) and Jowett was only 28 years of age yet he held the Manningham ward for fourteen years. Little did the young Jowett realise that he was about to 'step up' from being a 'half time' mill lad to a cabinet minister in Britain's first labour government after leaving school at 13!

Towards the end of 1890 a historic strike took place at Manningham Mills. The owner Mr Samuel Lister (later to become Lord Masham) wished for his workers to take a reduction in wages. A consequent meeting held at St George's hall on behalf of the locked out employees attracted a crowd of 3,000 and many others not able to get in and being driven away by police. A further meeting between strikers and the police led to serious rioting with many being injured. Infantry with fixed bayonets created a barrier across Tyrrel Street.

A further meeting of protest was held at Peckover Walks near the centre of Bradford and attracted estimated crowds of over 83,000. Fred Jowett was one of the speakers and the strikers received public sympathy. The strike went on a further nineteen weeks. The Independent Labour Party was formed in 1893 as a direct result of the strike and became the forerunner of the British Labour Party. Jowett, during the next fifteen years served socialism on the municipal stage funded by the members of I.L.P. who raised amongst themselves the sum of two pounds a week so Frederick Jowett could draw a wage and fully serve his constituents, during this span of time he undoubtedly did more for his citizens than any other person who had the honour of serving the local council. His achievements were endless.

In 1904 Bradford City Council decided to provide free school meals for all local school children. This move was inspired by Jowett and in 1906 after being elected MP for Bradford he was responsible for bringing onto the statute book the Education Act which enabled local authorities across the country to provide free school meals to all children whose background was poor. Bradford Council followed up this measure by providing school health checks for children, a midwifery service, and free meals for nursing and expectant mothers in certain areas and fire alarm boxes on streets before the advent of the telephone.

Housing was still a big problem so Jowett used his powers of persuasion to alleviate the problem. Bradford's biggest slum was Longlands, just off Westgate, which housed many Irish workers. Rows upon rows of soot covered back to back houses with brick yards and middens were in fact prisons for their tenants. These Irish workers had large families and were declared an insanitary area. After a three year fight the Longlands slum was cleared. This was deemed Jowett's greatest achievement. Jowett now turned his attention to the dreaded anthrax, the 'wool sorters disease'. The local trade's council and chamber of commerce applied jointly for a special code of rules to protect wool combers. A code of rules for the handing of dangerous wools was brought into force the following year 1900.

In terms of education the school board was now educating over 40,000 scholars and many were attending evening classes. St Bede's Roman Catholic school opened in Drewton Street and four years later in 1904 moved to Heaton Hall. Welfare reform pressed up unabated and small payments to outpatients of the eye and ear hospital were abolished. An old age pension scheme was created by the state and a committee elected by the council had to fulfil its undertakings.

In 1910 there were still 51 cases of anthrax in the Yorkshire textile industry, nine of these cases proving fatal. Dr Durich, a Home Office bacteriologist and Dr Bell, a Hallfield Road practitioner thankfully put an end to anthrax in the woollen industry. By 1933 there were only eight cases and only one was fatal, such was the improvement.

Jowett had pursued his pension for senior citizens for twenty years and eventually this came about with five shillings for both man and wife but only to be paid if not more than eight shillings a week came from other sources, a severe but dreaded means test!

The unemployment and health insurance act of 1911 was soon to follow. This hardworking politician was made alderman in 1909 and was also a J.P. He first contested parliament in 1900 but was defeated by 41 votes. Eventually he won a seat as MP in 1906 and followed this up by winning again in 1910. He eventually lost his seat in 1918 but served the constituency of East Bradford in 1922. At this point Ramsey McDonald gave him a seat in the Labour cabinet. He was steadfast to the I.L.P. and this was ultimately his downfall. He lost his seat in 1931 and after retiring lived on and annuity of £100. He died on February 1st 1944 never having received the full recognition locally but was noted for his integrity and oratory.

Chapter 14

Social Reformer Margaret McMillan

Another pioneer of social change at the time was Margaret McMillan who was born in 1860 into a middle class family. Margaret trained as a governess and tried to improve educational and health access to children of the industrial slums. Although Margaret was educated very well she suffered from deafness in her early years but recovered and became well-schooled in religious terms and travelling abroad. She thought along the lines of socialism and went to work amongst the poor of the east end of London and set about acquiring 'equality for all'. Ultimately she lost her paid position in London.

A new political party was arising in 1893 – this was the national Independent Labour Party and was formed in Bradford. Margaret used the opportunity to make regular visits to Bradford and gave speeches at Peckover Street off Leeds road and obtained a reputation as a good speaker. She was offered a job full time to further socialism but with no salary. Margaret, together with her sister Rachel lodged at 49 Hanover square off Manningham Lane, a plaque exists there even today stating that this fine educational reformer once lived there. She immediately threw herself into her work and the Sunday meetings of the ILP drew large audiences and were something akin to modern day evangelical meetings….

In 1894 she was invited to become an ILP candidate and agreed to stand for the East Ward, and won narrowly. In late 1894 she attended the school board and was duly elected to the education committee. For seven years she worked tirelessly to improve the conditions for school children. This was achieved although she was not very popular with the management after attacking the 'half time system'. She worked so hard that her health suffered. In 1902 she resigned from her seat on the school board. The poor children's lot was advanced because of her actions.

She stated 'all children are mine' and Bradford was described as 'The city of my heart'. The first school meal system opened at Green Lane School off Lumb Lane, shortly afterwards the headmaster of this school would have been J B Priestley's father. Improved medical facilities and school clinics became common place. All this was brought about by a remarkable woman who even today is remembered by a college of further education named in her honour

Chapter 15

Undercliffe Cemetery 'The Highgate of the North'

The 25 acre burial ground of Undercliffe cemetery is rightly called the Highgate of the North, perched high on a cliff overlooking Bradford. In the summer of 1851 the area was bought at auction for £3,400 pounds and in 1854 the process of burials began. The prominent souls who are buried here reflect Bradford's importance in the Victorian era. The amazing Illingworth mausoleum shows how this textile family progressed from the Providence mill in Tetley Street to the larger Whetley Mill on Thornton Road. Another amazing fact shows the Illingworth family remembered their dead worldwide through overseas inscriptions. Some gravestones at Undercliffe hold inscriptions to persons not buried there; some of these persons were buried in the four corners of the world, or even at sea. But the Bradford pioneering spirit has not been forgotten. Internments continued unabated with prominent figures competing for burial plots, jockeying for social position almost. It must be remembered that Bradford's population had been increasing at a phenomenal rate but Undercliffe remained the only private cemetery in the area. Huge corteges made their solemn march past the parish church of St Peter up church bank and then up to Undercliffe. The famous figures buried here include the Illingworth's, Sir Jacob Behrens and Sir Titus Salt, all of whom were textile merchants along with professional persons and social reformers of the highest order. The headstones and stone used in the cemetery were all quarried locally. As time progressed the graveyard fell into a state of disrepair and was bought by a Baildon developer in 1975 for £5. The graveyard had been desecrated by vandals and graffiti merchants. A steering group was formed called the friends of Undercliffe cemetery. Great improvements were made thanks to a body of unemployed men, about 65 in total who have restored the resting place to its former glory. The great and good can rest easy once again in their sombre sleep now this vital piece of history has been returned to its former greatness. Today 124,000 souls are buried there which also include Bradford's first wool Baron Swithin Anderson and the first Lord Mayor of Bradford, Sir John Arthur Godwin (1907).

The main Promenade through Undercliffe cemetery

Plots down the centre promenade were much more expensive.

Chapter 16

The Italians in Bradford

In Italy in the 1870s work was in short supply, poverty and dried up villages forced many people to move to Bradford and other industrial cities in England where work was said to be abundant and word got around that Bradford in particular was booming with work for many hands. Over a period of forty years or so to 1920 the Italians came in their thousands and many Italians worked in the iron foundries making castings for textile machinery whilst others hired barrel organs with two monkeys visiting certain parts of the city and obtaining donations for their services. The remaining immigrants worked in textiles and the selling of ice cream.

The Italians generally settled in the Otley Road area and this became known as 'Little Italy'. Many Italians intermarried with Irish Catholics who lived lower down Otley Road. Before the rush of the Italian immigrants, Italian architects had visited Bradford purchasing tons of local Bradford stone and exporting it back to their homeland to make palaces and churches. Many fine buildings still stand today in Bradford with much influence derived from Italian style, including the Town Hall and Law Russell House at the bottom of Leeds Road. Bradford had a culture of its own which is still evident today.

Probably the first Italian man of any note was Joseph Cadameteri who arrived in 1865, he was eighteen years old and started an ice cream business which enabled him to father fourteen children, and these children naturally followed him into the ice cream business which is still going today by the name of Caddy's Ices.

A cursory glance through the Bradford telephone directory will show the Italians are still present in the area today. When mentioning the Italians in Bradford the Fattorini's must be mentioned because without them the story would be incomplete. Antonio Fattorini originated from Bellagio on the banks of Lake Como in Lombardy in 1797.

He attempted, with other young men, to fight in the Napoleonic war but arrived too late to see any action. While some of his friends returned home Antonio pressed on for England to seek his fortune. He arrived in Dewsbury and started selling pots and pans until 1827. He then opened a stall in Leeds Briggate and gradually moved to Bradford. He noticed Bradford had only five jewellery shops and through Antonio's son John, a watchmaker, they offered free credit to the working men of Bradford to purchase pocket watches which were needed with the large expansion of office and factories.

The business continued to grow and finally turned to mail order which led to the creation of Empire Stores and Grattan. This was bought about by the Northern Trading Company based at 20 Sackville Street in the centre of Bradford and its agents all over the north of England as the company name suggest. In March 1859 Antonio died aged 63. So successful was he that his name was known all over the West Riding. The family remained in the public eye and manufactured the current F.A cup in 1911 for 50 guineas with Bradford City being the first winners. The family's association with the business continued unabated until 1991.

Chapter 17

Irish Society in Bradford

The Irish immigrants of the 1800's can be rightly regarded as the first working immigrant community in Bradford. They began to arrive in the 1820's although the main bulk of these families followed in 1845 following the potato famine. They settled in the inner city areas of Goit Side, Longlands and Wapping. Bradford already had an army of unemployed and did not welcome the arrival, their religion as Roman Catholics caused further problems as this was then classified as the 'old religion'. The jobs that were on offer to them were in the textile industry but conditions and pay were abysmal. The Catholics, after a great struggle were able to open their first place of worship in 1825 in what was known as St. Mary's Chapel on East Parade, nestling in the shadows of the Cathedral/Parish church. St Mary's eventually became a church and it still stands today, although no longer in use as a place of worship. It almost became a social centre where after mass contacts were obtained to find jobs in the construction industry. This giant Building stands silent today.

St Patricks in Sedgefield Terrace opened in 1853 but still the Irish suffered huge discrimination. The housing accommodation that they were able to obtain was terrible, with an average of eight people living in one room and consequently hygiene was very bad. Many children died in their early years. Many types of housing and retail work was denied to these people but still the immigrants were grateful for small mercy's and felt there was no turning back.

It was estimated that by the middle of the nineteenth century 10,000 Irish people lived in Bradford but many were not able to speak English, and were illiterate. Anti-Catholic riots broke out in the 1850's and 1860's but since this brief violence the Irish Catholics have assimilated into local society and beyond. Today there are an amazing 45,000 people estimated with ancestry connections in the Bradford area.

Chapter 18 - As Time Goes By

The coming of the Asians

Immigrants have been coming to Bradford for the last 200 years but none have made such a modern impact as the people from South Asia. Many minority groups such as the Guajarati's from North West India, the Afghans from the North West Frontier, the Bangladeshi's, the Punjabi's from the Indian/Pakistan border, the Kenya/Uganda Asians and most profoundly the Mirpur's from the mountain villages near Kashmir. The first Asians to arrive in Bradford came in the 1930's after jumping ship and ending up in munitions factories or more specifically the West Yorkshire textile mills. They settled at the bottom of Little Horton Lane in the houses around Howard Street and were inevitably young single males. Their idea was to work hard, earn as much money as possible in a short time and return home, but it did not turn out that way. The immigrants were welcomed with 'open arms' by local textile employers who were going through the process of installing new machinery which would have to be used constantly to obtain a profit. The Young men who put themselves forward for this type of work suffered hardship and racism and also dietary problems. It must have been a culture shock seeing only factory mill chimneys belching out smoke but they stuck to their task even among the cold and freezing days of winter. In the early 1960's immigration controls were tightened and the young men brought their families over. The Asians started buying up houses in the inner city wards but in the last 10 years or so have seen a wholesale movement to the better residential suburbs. Whilst jobs in public transport, foundries and textiles have declined, the Asians have been quick to enter the self-employment market and particularly corner shops, taxis and the restaurant trade. For many people there has been no choice but to set up in business or face unemployment. Cinemas, shops of all kinds, garages, travel agents, banks and legal offices have transpired in the last 30 years. Co-operation amongst themselves and self-help has allowed the Asians to prosper and reach new dimensions. It could be said that the Asians greatest achievement in Bradford was the installation of a Lord Mayor, Councillor Mohammed Ajeeb in 1985 who commanded great respect, not only from the Asian society, but most sections of the Bradford population. Other Asian mayors were soon to follow.

Councillor Mohammed Ajeeb, The first Asian Lord Mayor elected in Bradford In 1985, since awarded a CBE in 2001.

The Store with a Friendly Welcome

Busbys became, along with Brown and Muff, the top department stores in Bradford's heyday. Ernest Busby was the original founder of Busby stores in 1908 at a different location from the famous Manningham Lane site. The original premises were located at Kirkgate where Ernest purchased two shops for just over £3,000. This gentleman of some considerable foresight had just left the Owen and Owen Ltd of Liverpool after completing an apprenticeship with a certain Matthew Rose and completed his indentures without pay as was the practice at the time.

Along came the Great War after which Ernest's three sons came to join the business. Another store was purchased in Ilkley in 1918 and generally things were looking up. Now it was the roaring twenties and the Bradford haberdashery store was continuing to prosper because of the great trade cycle running in Bradford's favour in the textile trade. Ernest now felt that the stores in Kirkgate had outlived their usefulness and looked for larger premises at the edge of the city. A suitable location was located on Manningham Lane. Even during the depression of the 1930s trade continued to grow. In what now was a department store where 800 staff were employed, the store was family orientated and the management saw that all requisites were met. Busby's sales became legendary with hordes of people queuing patiently for bargains at hand.

Even today Bradford's senior citizens recollect fond memories of this unique store. Ernest Busby died in 1957 aged 87, a year later Busby's continued in name only since they had merged with Debenhams. In 1973 Debenhams took complete control. Five years later Debenhams decided to close the premises and demolish the structure but a huge fire destroyed the premises saving the demolition men the expense. A sad end to a glorious era!

Reservoirs and their importance to Bradford

In the late nineteenth century Bradford had a problem with its rapid industrial expansion. Its continued growth in textile mills and population explosion created a demand for water. Luckily a forward thinking soul was in evidence. A certain Anthony Gadie decided revenue should be raised by an additional figure to be placed on the general rates however small (thought to be 1d) The location of such reservoirs was to be at the head of the Nidd Valley above Pateley Bridge about 30 miles from Bradford.

Gouthwaite compensation reservoir was created two miles in length and water to be released into the Nidd when water level was low. A Scottish firm was engaged in 1893 – John Best and son. Eight years later the project was complete. The cost was £240,000 to Bradford council. Higher up the valley another reservoir was to be completed called Angram and again built by John Best and his employees. Materials were secured a HQ based in Lofthouse, they were then sent by rail at Pateley Bridge some miles down the valley. A village was built by Best a couple of years after the start of the project including a school a church and canteens. The reservoir was unusual as it was not of standard construction but made of concrete pillars and rough stones, this was a slow process with winter weather often taking hold and dragging out the completion until 1917, the cost being over £372,000. A further reservoir scheme started in 1913 to be called Scar House in the same higher Nidd Valley but was not completed until 1935. The old Haden Carr reservoir was submerged and the work began. By 1929 about 700 men were working on the project. The general strike of 1926 did not affect the progress and by the summer of 1935 the site was complete.

The Bradford Press

Bradford's only daily circulation is held by the Telegraph & Argus which has held this name since 1947 but whose circulation has declined somewhat in the last twenty five years.

It once held circulation figures around the 100,000 mark on a daily basis. Its circulation area covers Skipton to Heckmondwike, at one time copies were sent on trains from Forster Square train station to Morecambe to cater for Bradford's huge retired population by the sea. The actual first newspaper in Bradford was the Bradford Observer, a weekly paper just before the Victorian era commenced.

In 1868 Bradford's first daily newspaper started, the Bradford Daily Telegraph which just happens to be related to its current daily sister paper, the Telegraph & Argus.

Other papers followed, the Bradford Daily Argus (soon to become the Yorkshire Evening Argus) all competing against each other until 1926 when the Telegraph & Argus merged with the Westminster Press. The competition then fell away. The local press is known to be keen on sport of all kinds and until fairly recently 'The Sporting Pink' was published on Saturday evenings for sports fans with full results for that day and full coverage of games involving local teams. This paper was released on an eager public within an hour of the Saturday afternoon games finishing and therefore held a tight deadline.

Sadly circulation of the 'Pink' declined and it ceased to be printed in the early nineteen eighties.

Bradford and its Association with Hangmen

James Berry was known all over the world as a hangman and one of Bradford's first practitioners of the sordid trade. As one of Britain's modern executioners, he put to death some 134 men and women and was also known as the first hangman to be literate.

He was born in Heckmondwike and born thirteenth in a family of eighteen in 1852. He was classified a man of normal working class virtue and he plied the trade of policeman in Bradford from 1874. On the death of a certain William Marwood a Lincolnshire cobbler, Berry became a student of the science of sudden death. Berry took to the task of executioner if only for economic reasons and carried it on like a business. James only received his position after some intense competition from 1,400 men.

He began his career in 1884 and his home at 1 Bilton Place which became known as 'The Executioners Office'. Government reports asked the hangman to err on the side of caution and lengthen the rope rather than shortening it if any doubt entered the executioners mind, however Berry would shorten the rope if he considered the crime serious enough so as to ensure the person strangled. James Berry retired as a hangman in1891 after nightmares continued to haunt him. He took to drink, entered music hall and became a member of a Christian revival group .He is buried in plot/grave 781 in Lidget Green cemetery. The tradition of hangmen was to continue in Bradford through a certain Albert Pierrepoint. The Pierrepoint's were an amazing family, father, son and uncle, Henry,

Albert and Thomas each at one time held the position of hangman of England. James Billington succeeded Berry as executioner but after a serious of botched execution Henry Pierrepoint wrote to the Home Secretary asking for the position of assistant to Billington, however he was turned down without an interview but this was a mistake as prison staff at Manchester Strangeways prison assumed he had applied for a job as prison warder. Eventually he went for a fortnights training in Newgate prison and between 1901 and 1910 he executed 110 people.

Henry died in 1922. Duly, Thomas, Albert's uncle took over the sordid trade. Albert was now growing up and took a variety of jobs including a bookies runner. The executioners' job appealed to him, particularly the idea of travel as very few people in 1920 had a car. Adventure got the better of Albert and with his family connections duly obtained the post of executioner. Records show he executed 435 sad souls between 1932 and 1955. The family as a whole dispatched 834 persons from this life. The Pierrepoint's considered themselves as carrying out a public duty. Albert was a Clayton boy born at 5 Green End but now time was passing by and the Pierrepoint family dynasty was coming to an end and capital punishment was finally abolished in 1969.

Albert Pierrepoint

Bradford Park Avenue F.C.

The Park Avenue sports ground opened in 1880 as a dual purpose operation for cricket and rugby sporting clubs. In the early 1900's association football arrived and took a strong foothold, not only in Bradford, but all over the West Riding of Yorkshire. Within a couple of years Bradford Park Avenue F.C. under the chairmanship of Harry Briggs were riding high with an international match staged at Park Avenue which drew an attendance of over 25,000! A double sided main stand had been erected, one side for football and the other side for cricket. In the corner of the football ground was the famous changing room or 'dolls house' as it was known, similar in design to the Fulham AFC structure at Craven Cottage in fashionable west London.

By 1913/14 Park Avenue were in the first division, every clubs dream, and achieved a respectable ninth place. They had reached their sporting zenith apart from glory days with cup runs. On one occasion after the Second World War they entertained Manchester City losing 1-3 and nobody gave them a chance for the second leg but Len Shackleton ran riot trouncing the boys in blue with an 8-2 win! Even the amazing England international goalkeeper Frank Swift and England former centre half Sam Barkas could not stop the deluge. A huge crowd left the game in disbelief. Avenue continued their giant killing exploits in 1949 by taking Manchester United to two replays before being soundly thrashed 5-0. The wind had been taken out of Avenue's sails and it all went pear shaped after 1950. So much so that after the sale of Kevin Hector in 1966 Avenue had to apply for re-election to the football league on a number of occasions in the late nineteen sixties before accepting their fate and entering the Northern Premier League.

After a further 3 years Avenue fell into terminal decline, so much so that they moved across the city to Valley Parade and the home of their greatest rivals Bradford City A.F.C. The rise in Avenues rent was astronomical and both the Inland Revenue and the local council in effect took the club into voluntary liquidation.

Other ideas were mooted for the use of the Park Avenue ground but nothing actually transpired and most of the ground remained semi derelict. Demolition came about in 1980. The ghosts of many fine and talented footballers will continue to haunt this ground and live in the memory of older Bradfordians for many years to come. The only positive note came about in 1988 when the club was reformed and due to many promotions were within striking distance of the football league only to hit bad times and be relegated on two occasions. Only time will tell if Avenue re-enter the football league once again, but I for one wish them well in their future endeavours.

Manningham's Hidden Secrets

Manningham is just north of the city centre. Unfortunately in modern times it had become associated with drugs, prostitution, high unemployment and other associated ills. This however has not always been the case, as in other sections of this book Manningham was the home area to the crème de la crème of Bradford society up until the 1950's. Many famous men and women have been born in its boundaries but the most sinister and mysterious would be Ernest Wilhelm Hans Bohle, Born in 1903 to Hermann and Toni Bohle, at 14 Bertram Road. He apparently weighed 15lbs at birth and was fed undiluted goat's milk and walked unaided at 9 months. At the age of 3 he left Bradford never to return. His father obtained a work position in South Africa. Ernest eventually gravitated to Cologne in Germany to study commerce. Ernest was captivated by the German National Socialist Workers Party and its leader – Adolf Hitler. Hitler made him a minister with responsibilities for the three million abroad to swear allegiance to the Thousand Year Reich. Bohle renounced his British citizenship in 1939 which saved him going to the gallows for treason. In 1941 he claimed he helped Rudolph Hess come to Britain, but this was never proven. In 1945 following Germany's defeat he was sentenced to five years for being a member of the German secret service but was released before his term expired. If Germany had won the war Bohle would have signed Winston Churchill's arrest warrant, but thankfully this never happened and Bohle faded into obscurity. In recent times St Pauls Road was the meeting place for the Baader-

Meinhof terrorist group. Sir Edward Appleton, the scientist and Noble prize winner lived at 64 Hanover Square in 1901. As you proceed down Oak Lane and turn right into Roseberry Road you will see a building on the right hand side in poor state of repair. This belonged to Henry VIII's head horseman and is probably Bradford's oldest building after the Cathedral. Oliver North of Contra Deal fame, his grandfather lived on Belravia Place off Green Lane before setting sail from Liverpool at the end of the Victorian era.

The Yorkshire Ripper

Many grisly murders have been committed through the course of time in the Bradford area, but no one born in the Bradford district has acquired such notoriety as the man to become known as the Yorkshire Ripper, Peter Sutcliffe. Sutcliffe's reign of terror began in July 1975 when Anna Rogulski was found battered in Alice Street in Keighley, luckily she survived her ordeal. A month later Olive Smelt was discovered with horrific head injuries, like Rogulski, she survived but lived to carry the scars of her ordeal. Some months later another victim was clinically dispatched with macabre medical efficiency – Wilma Mc Cann and in turn this catalogue of violence went on to become Britain's biggest ever manhunt. Over a five year period 13 women died and four were maimed, mostly in red light districts of West Yorkshire, but respectable women also became victims. Police were bamboozled and had to use only the manual methods of detection available to them allowing the mass killer a free reign, during which, he slipped through their hands on more than one occasion. Forensic tests brought no results but they knew the killer had a rare blood group. In today's age of massive forensic advancement I feel sure the police would have been able to collar their man at a much earlier stage. Scotland Yard were brought in to assist the West Yorkshire force in November 1979. By that time women were terrified to walk the streets after dark alone and the pressure took its toll on George Oldfield, the Assistant Chief constable who suffered two heart attacks during the investigation.

Eventually Sutcliffe was captured in Sheffield after thousands of man hours spent by the local and national forces closed this lurid episode. Sutcliffe received twenty life sentences in 1981

Sutcliffe is by no means isolated in his feats – he was just carrying on the same sad spotlight of the Black Panther– Donald Neilson together with Bradford's association with hangmen will be forever etched in Bradford's sad demise in its past.

The Bradford City Fire Disaster May 11th 1985

Perhaps the greatest tragedy to strike Bradford in modern times occurred on a fateful day in May 1985. Bradford City AFC had five days previously secured the third division championship at Bolton, nine months of sweat and toil with many moments of fine attacking play to remember this team by. City were back in Division two for the first time since 1937. The city had come alive in football terms and the fans celebrated but that was quickly dispelled in a few short minutes that Saturday afternoon. A crowd of over 11,000 had gathered at Valley Parade to watch their heroes' parade the championship trophy. Tragedy struck all too quickly. The author himself attended the match standing in front of the old wooden stand. Turning my head around, I saw smoke rising quickly. Just where the smoke was coming from I could not distinguish. The smoke grew quickly into large flames which became uncontrollable eventually engulfing one side of the ground and taking 56 lives. The news became national headlines and quickly spread around the world. Success had turned to tragedy and football was put into perspective. The people of Bradford had to rally round their thoughts being with the deceased's loved ones. A special bond was created between players, fans and Bradfordians in general which was to serve the club well in the next fifteen years in their quest for higher grade football. Promotions came together with European matches, trips to Wembley and generally the big time 'Charlie's' were around. All these things would have been scoffed at a generation before by the Bradford supporting public considering only 1,200 people had turned out for an end of season game in 1981. A minutes silence at a match each May and a memorial service outside the City Hall together with a victim's roll call at the new main stand entrance shows the victims' families they will never be forgotten.

Bradford's Future

In the 1960's Bradford still possessed around 700 weavers, spinners, topmakers and textile merchants and with their demise went the 'old' Bradford. What is left of J B Priestley's old Bradford is still cherished by those old enough to remember. Applying for the European City of culture in 2008 Bradford fell far short of what was required according to the judges, who never set forth on the city and took misguided ideas and conceptions at least that is what I tell myself!

Did the judges know that Bradford has over 5,800 listed buildings, which is more than double of the eventual winners, Liverpool? Did four young men called the Beatles ever have anything to do with them making their selection? We will never know! The current word is regeneration, but the city appears to be one big building site judging by the cranes in place dotted around the city and its suburbs strategically. Many see Bradford with a great future and 2 billion pounds are being invested. The city was recently named the Unesco First city of Film with Los Angeles and Cannes. Bradfordians themselves are somewhat cynical and have heard it all before with many 'master plans' never getting off the ground! The planners had a certain fixation with water and created a lake in the city centre called City Park. I must admit to admiring it now its complete and it does seem to draw in the crowds regular, but we have numerous parks around the city being given to rack and ruin (and habitual drug users) and a Canal Road Master plan which will re-introduce the old canal which was closed down in 1922.It appears this will take over 10 years to complete. Figures currently available show an additional 55,000 jobs will be created over the next 10 years, this is good news together with the recent announcement that the Bradford area possesses one of the largest ownerships of Rolls Royce's in the country. Could Bradford be returning to some of its former glory? Can a New Jerusalem be created from the dark satanic mills? Only time will tell.

Chapter 19-Famous Bradfordians

Lost City (J B Priestley)

John Boynton Priestley was born at 34 Mannheim Road just off Toller lane in 1894 and a plaque still stands to mark the spot. The road has special significance for the author of this book as he also lived there for sixteen years and met the great man on one occasion. Priestley left the road himself at an early age and moved a short distance with his parents to Saltburn Place in 1904, but made many sentimental journeys back to Mannheim Road later in life when he had left Bradford.

Priestley's father, Jonathan was a schoolmaster and socialist of the old school who led a comfortable existence teaching at Belle Vue Grammar School and Head of the Green Lane School off Lumb Lane. His mother came from a poorer background and died soon after John's birth. John attended Whetley Lane Primary School, his father re married and John won a scholarship at Belle Vue Grammar School. John or Jack as he was later known left school and worked as a junior clerk at a company in the now gone Swan Arcade off Market Street... The work was dull but most teenagers at that age had no option, they ended up in the textile trade. Before 1914 Bradford handled 80% of the country's wool trade and was considered the most progressive city in the UK. Its earnings from textiles were 90 million pounds. London never entered Priestley's head and he was essentially a West Riding man who attended cultural activities of theatres and concert halls which would later influence his writing. In 1914 he had no option but to join the army at the advent of the First World War and after suffering injury he was to take no more part in active service. He was to resurface as a writer of great repute. John attended Cambridge in 1921 after he married Pat Tempest two years before. Within a couple of years he had published a number of books, his father was now dead and his wife Pat died of cancer leaving him with two children to look after. The number of new books continued and John remarried. Probably his new novel 'good companions' created the breakthrough that was needed, his seventeenth book, which reflected life at that time. 'Bruddersford' was first mentioned thinly disguised as his home city. Priestley was now bringing up a young family but could rest assured he would have no financial problems due to his large book sales.. He had now left his home city and continued his writing but Bradford never left him, it was always in his thoughts. 'When We Are Married' 1938, 'Bright Days' 1945 was soon to follow and described as his best work. 'Margin Released' 1962 looked back at his teenage years and 'The Clerk' 1966 in which he remembered his first dull job in Swan Arcade all those years before.

The countryside that surrounded Bradford which also included the dales also left an influence on him so much as to say in his youth he lived on some of the most enchanting countryside in England. 'English Journey' described the depression of the nineteen thirties and Priestley's journey through it taking in the cities of Southampton, Bristol and on to the Black Country surrounding Birmingham. From there he travelled east to Leicester and Nottingham, Northwards to West Riding and Lancashire and up to the Tyne area. From there he travelled some distance back south to the Norfolk Broads and on to Highgate in North London. At this point in his life he was derided by his fellow Bradfordians for deserting his home city for the south and his relationship with the local press was even less cordial. He was still the bluff Yorkshireman recalling his youth in a glamorous Bradford which stuck with him all his life. The many tram journeys down Toller Lane to the Sunbridge road terminus never left his mind. His 'lost City' went with him to his grave in 1984 after receiving the Order of Merit from the Queen at Buckingham Palace in 1977. His ashes are buried in the graveyard at Hubberholme church in Upper Wharfedale in his beloved Yorkshire Dales.

Bradford's Master Evangelical Preacher

In 1859 Smith Wigglesworth was born in Menston. By the time he was six years of age he was pulling turnips from morning till night. At seven he turned to working twelve hours a day in a textile mill in the footsteps of his father, a weaver. His mother and father were not interested in religion. At thirteen years of age the family moved to Bradford. If anything the family had leanings to the Wesleyan faith through Smiths grandmother, Bella. At thirteen years of age Smith was confirmed into the Church of England although the followers of Wesleyan were large in numbers in Yorkshire. For a while Smith embraced the Salvation Army but discipline here was very strong. Smith travelled around Liverpool preaching mainly to poor children. At twenty three years of age he returned to Bradford to marry a girl who he had become attached to in the Salvation Army, Polly, alias Mary Jane Featherstone who had left her strict parents and arrived in Bradford five years earlier. Polly was a fine speaker at religious meetings and bore Smith five children.

By 1883 Smith had a trade; he was a plumber and lived at 70 Victor Road, in Lower Heaton, an up and coming suburb. This was to be his home and base for the next sixty four years. The business of plumbing was so prosperous Smith had little time for preaching and also put pressure on his domestic life and marriage. After going through a difficult period in his life he came back to preaching with renewed vigour, speaking in tongues of fire. He opened the Bowland Street Mission just off Lumb Lane, opposite the Jewish reform Synagogue. He made miraculous healings and soon had a large following. One of his most famous converts was James Berry the public executioner. Berry happened to be based in Bradford and was contemplating suicide. His severe depression was lifted and Berry himself went on to convert five hundred souls. Smith travelled the world preaching in Switzerland, Norway, Denmark, Sweden and a multitude of other countries including Angola, Zaire (the Congo) and South Africa, he drew huge crowds converted many souls and wrote books including 'Ever increasing faith'.

He was still a straight talking Yorkshire man but his own health began to deteriorate and he took years off his ministry. The experience certainly affected him and he became gentle in his mannerisms The master preacher converted and preached for another fifteen years but considering he cured thousands across the world from medical ailments and handicaps, he was never able to cure his daughter Alice's deafness. They say God works in mysterious ways but was the creator trying to tell him something? The extremely cold weather finally got the better of Smith and on Twelfth March 1947 he died after a prolonged illness and was buried in the family plot at Nab Wood cemetery along with his beloved wife 'Polly' and his son George. Sad to say there is no plaque outside 70 Victor Road today, yet many make the pilgrimage to see his home and grave from around the world.

Vic Feather- Trade Unionist

Vic Feather was born in 1908, the son of a lorry driver. He was educated at Undercliffe School and the Hanson. In 1923 he left school and joined Bradford Co-op as a delivery boy and soon joined the shop workers union. Such was his political affiliations that further work came his way in the form of union subscription collector. Being a fine orator he quickly rose through the political ranks and in 1937 joined the staff of the Trade Union Congress and beat off 350 applicants to secure the position. In 1947 he became assistant general secretary of the T.U.C and in 1970 took the chief role.

Retirement came four years later and he was made Lord Feather of Bradford. The work achieved through his political leanings gave young modern day worker's rights they take for granted. This was not achieved without many years of toil and struggle on the union's behalf and gave British workers decent standards of living. Sadly work took its toll on Vic's life and he passed away in the summer of 1976 but not before he changed many people's lives.

George W Bush and his Descendants

At the time of writing the once world's most powerful man is not aware of his Bradford descendants. James Uncles, born in Bradford in 1794 is the great, great, great, great grandfather of George W. Bush. Mr Uncles married Elizabeth Criswell in 1816. Their daughter married Thomas Sheldon whose son, Robert wed Mary Elizabeth Butler. Consequently their daughter Flora Sheldon married Samuel Prescott Bush and the rest is history, as they say. Mr Bush's political career has been mired in controversy but I do not wish to take any political stance. He appears to have a sense of humour, something very strange considering he has Yorkshire blood flowing through his veins! Remember his "Yo Blair" during an international summit?

Bradford's Fiery Cricketer

David Bairstow was born in 1951 and hailed from the Bradford Moor area. Cricket figured highly in his teenage years and he gradually progressed through the local leagues and his debut for Yorkshire came about in strange circumstances.

In 1970 he was due to make his first class Yorkshire debut, fittingly at Park Avenue, his home turf, against Gloucestershire but his A level exams coincided on the same day at Hanson Grammar School. It was decided the only option was to commence his exams at 6 AM at a special sitting.

He then duly proceeded to Park Avenue and soon after putting on his cricket whites took a catch behind the wicket, which must have increased his confidence no end. David was the first schoolboy to be chosen for the white rose county. This red haired character has been described as a jovial character, positive in his outlook and held a broad Yorkshire accent. His strolling to the wicket showed his confidence, whirling his bat through the air and must have been a frightening sight to the opposition but made him popular with Yorkshire cricket followers who knew they would always receive 110% effort. He went on to claim over 1,000 catches and over 12,000 runs. He was tragically found dead at his home in Marton-Cum Grafton in North Yorkshire in 1998 at the young age of 46 but you can be rest assured he lived life to the full and there was never a dull moment when he was around.

The Gentle Giant

On the eighth of February 2006 Bradford's gentle giant passed away namely Jack Taylor or as some locals had called him 'Fat Jack'. He had lived a quiet life in the Manningham area and became a recluse shunning his superstar status in Germany where he had starred with Jackie Chan in the Kung Fu movies.

His fifty stone frame, seventy one inch waist and eighty inch hips meant you could not miss him in the street and ultimately led him staying indoors for thirty years. Jack had to go ex-directory due to been inundated with his legion of fans constantly ringing him up and in Germany being compared to the Spice Girls and the Royal family in terms of popularity.

The ex-wrestler and security guard had been advised to take special exercise by his doctor but Jack stated he never got round to it. In 2006 at the age of 60 he met his maker. A heart attack brought his life to an abrupt end. A special service was arranged at St Patrick's Roman Catholic Church, Sedgefield Terrace off Westgate where a reinforced double coffin was employed with eight pallbearers who struggled somewhat to lift this amazing gentleman. He lies buried in Rawdon cemetery.

Professor Joseph Wright

At the time of Joseph's birth in 1855 not many people in the West Riding were versed in the English standard Language but this was to change through Fosters Education Act in 1870 and at a later date the introduction of Joseph Wright's dialect dictionary. Joseph was born at Thackley and began work as a 'donkey boy' in the quarries of Idle at six years of age. His duties involved working ten hours a day driving a donkey cart carrying quarryman's tools to the nearest blacksmith. The blacksmith paid him 1s 6d a week while quarrymen paid him 1d each.

At seven years of age he started to work in Salts Mill, although under the legal minimum age, he became a doffer. His wages were three shillings and sixpence per week. He was known as a 'half timer' working alternate mornings and afternoons whilst trying to obtain an education provided by Sir Titus Salt. This was the only time Joseph received free education and never in his life did he receive a full day of education. Joseph left Salts Mill in 1868 and became fully literate in 1870. At this point in his life he became a fully-fledged wool sorter but yearned for further education, this came via The Mechanics Institute in Bradford to be followed at a later stage by night school at the Yorkshire College in Leeds each evening after work. This entailed him walking eight miles in each direction, getting home and then straight back to work next morning! As time passed by capital was accumulated and Joseph resigned from his job and studied philosophy at Heidelberg University in Germany. A doctorate became forthcoming in 1885. In 1891 he was given the task of compiling the English dialect dictionary whereby his dialect work involved processing and editing about 1 million notes. This took fourteen years to complete and two thousand pounds of Joseph's money as no publisher could be found. Such was the success of this publication that today this remains the standard reference of English Language throughout the planet.

 A high position came as Joseph obtained the position of Corpus Christi Professor of Comparative Philology at Oxford University, a post he held until 1924. Degrees from fellow universities came his way and he became Vice President of the Royal Society of Literature. What an amazing Journey for the illiterate boy from Thackley who yearned for knowledge to better life for himself, his relatives and his family. The dour pragmatism of Joseph shone through to beat almost impossible odds.

A Fine Reformer- Mathew Balme

Matthew Balme is another man not well known locally although he strove to improve the conditions for children working in local mills and factories. Matthew was born in 1813 in Idle to a family who had lived around Bradford since the sixteenth century. He began his working life as a teacher. He changed professions and worked as a clerk in local government and from 1858 registered births and deaths in North Bradford. Factory reform turned out to be the real zeal in his life and he became a great friend of Richard Oastler, another locally born reformer but who became better known than Matthew. Factory committees were formed with local branches in the West Riding basically to protect child workers and their hours of work. In 1838 Matthew became a local secretary of such a branch and complained against a local company overworking children at odds, against the Factory Act 1833. In the course of his work he briefed the Parliamentary leaders, including Lord Ashley and continued to apply pressure by stating in 1846 'That the people of this vast and influential Riding would never became satisfied until this bill becomes law' The motion was narrowly defeated but the next year in 1847 the bill was finally passed. Matthew died in 1884 and is buried in the grounds of the church of Saint Wilfred at Calverley, where a memorial was erected by many friends including W E Forster and two thousand factory workers. The stones stated:

'Defend the poor and fatherless, Do justice to the afflicted and needy'

Jim Laker - Cricketer Extraordinaire

Born in 1922 at 36 Norwood Road Frizinghall and educated at Salts Boys High School, this amazing off spinner was rejected when attending cricket trials for his native Yorkshire after playing for Saltaire cricket club. In 1946 Surrey, Yorkshires arch rivals from the south took advantage of the situation and signed him on a special registration. This turned out to be Yorkshires undoing over the next decade. Laker returned to his home county for the 1950 test trial and recorded amazing figures of 8 wickets for 2 runs, surely never to be surpassed! His amazing form continued with Surrey who achieved 7 county championship titles in the 1950's in consecutive summers at Yorkshire's expense. To many he will always be remembered for the 1956 Test match at Old Trafford against the Australians taking 19 of the 20 wickets for just 90 runs. During his career he took almost 2,000 first class wickets and 1950 being his finest season with 166 wickets at just over 15 runs per wicket. Surely he must be one of the all-time greats in the cricket world. A very humble and easy going man, the likes of which, we will probably never see again. Yorkshire cricket club will be kicking themselves for allowing him to slip through their grasp but Bradford never forgot him and aptly named a thoroughfare in his honour.

The Legend of Trevor Foster MBE

The word 'legend' is branded about far more loosely today but this man was a sure fire legend, judging by the honours that were bestowed upon him. How do you describe a man who had honours from every section of society? The Queen, The Pope, the City of Bradford, Bradford University, Rugby league, the list goes on…..

Born in 1914 in Newport South Wales, he was the youngest of six children and he soon entered into Ruby Union for Newport schoolboys and left school at fourteen years of age. The scouts from the large rugby league clubs in the north of England soon became aware of his talents. Trevor was heavily influenced by his father and had a strict upbringing, including a private catholic convent education. Gradually Trevor's father lost his sight and died putting a great deal of weight on this young man's shoulders. Trevor was soon close to winning his first Welsh cap when Bradford Northern came forward with an offer Trevor could not refuse.

In September 1938 he moved north for a fee of £400, the largest fee at the time for a Welsh forward. He quickly adapted to his new way of life in the textile city, as Bradford shared many similarities to his home town and therefore became his 'home from home'. The tall athletic young man soon established a place in the Bradford team until the outbreak of war. Naturally, he was conscripted and on returning to civilian life he led his team to three successive Wembley finals in 1947, 1948 and 1949, winning two out of the three. He toured Australia and retired from the game in 1955.

Northern went into decline and the club had to be reformed after a public meeting at St Georges Hall. Naturally, Trevor was involved in the rescue operation.. Trevor in the meantime had married June Unsworth in 1949 and raised a family spending most of his time in the Heaton district under the shadow of Lister's Mill. He became involved in many local charities after he retired from his position as Education Welfare Officer (formerly the school bobby!).

In 2001 he was fittingly awarded an MBE, accompanied by his children.

This was a fitting honour for a true gentleman. He gave hope to others by unstintingly offering his time and advice. Such was the life of Trevor Foster who died in 2005 after having a Bradford road named after him.

John Braine (Man at the top)

John was born in 1922 on Sedgefield Terrace off Westgate opposite Saint Patrick's church. His father was a very calm Methodist and his mother was a strong Irish Catholic. He was brought up in the Roman Catholic faith and he was educated at St Bede's Grammar School. Living at Thackley, he left School in 1938 without qualifications and worked in a number of 'dead end jobs' until in 1940 he received the position of library assistant at the old Bingley library.

At this point in his life he became ill with tuberculosis and much time was spent at the Grassington sanatorium, which in turn led to him becoming a freelance writer as his independent way of thinking came to the fore. This therefore shows Bradford was a city with a character all of its own. On a recurrence of tuberculosis he was re admitted to the Grassington sanatorium and during his stay he began writing his novel 'Room at The Top' although this novel had been given two previous names before arriving at this most famous one. It received rave reviews in the national newspapers. John loved the praise and thrived on it. He was, at that time, living on £13 a week as a librarian near Barnsley. His earnings shot up considerably to possibly £1,000 per week and this enabled him to return to Bingley and buy a large house by the side of his beloved moors. The blockbuster novel reflect the social change going on generally in England and proved to be the most striking novel for a generation selling 35,000 hardback copies in its first year. Joe Lampton, the main character in the novel was played on screen by the late Laurence Harvey, he became the first anti-hero. The name of the town for the setting of the novel was thinly disguised Warley, but was a West Riding Mill town, probably Bradford or Bingley. The film was made on location in 1958.

A further 12 novels followed but only 'Life At The Top' made any great impression probably due to the fact that social change that had taken place over the intervening five years and radicalism had been accepted.

The jealous God, The Crying Game and Stay with Me Till Morning all followed. His last novel, written in 1985, These Golden Days, was described as a minor classic.

He retired to the south of England, never to be the same and coming up against a series of problems including a bank overdraft, large tax bills and a broken marriage. He influenced a generation of writers including West Riding born Stanley Barstow who wrote 'Kind of Loving'. John remarked to his old school pupils in 1958 that they should get educational qualifications behind them as they might not be as tough or lucky as the author in his bohemian lifestyle. John Braine died in 1986.

James Ashley 'Salt Jim'

'Salt Jim' was certainly a character of Victorian Bradford. He could be seen wandering the streets of Bradford carrying a bar of salt, supposedly under his filthy jacket. Under this pretext, when arrested by the local constabulary for begging he had the alibi he was a salt trader.

Everybody in Bradford knew him by name and to the man in the street he was better known than civic dignitaries. 'Salt Jim' died in 1911 at the old Bradford workhouse in Little Horton Lane and the medical establishment declared him a half-wit. Little did they know Jim had over two hundred pounds in his bank account when he died, which was equivalent to 3 to 4 years wages for a manual worker. A cheeky but very shrewd man in my opinion!

The Great Gambler

Joseph Hobson Jagger was born in Shelf, a little village close to the Halifax border of Bradford in 1830. He was a textile engineer by trade working at Henry Bottomleys, Clough Mills in his home village. The story goes that he set off on horseback in 1875 on his annual two weeks holiday and was heading for the south of France. Eventually, he arrived at his destination some two days later after using the train service to Monaco. After approaching a casino out of sheer curiosity he saw roulette being played for the very first time. He apparently distrusted anything not manufactured in England and spotted a potential fault in the roulette cylinders which were of a rough construction. Joseph placed his first bet on July 7th 1875 and began winning on a regular basis. Eventually he attracted the attention of the casino security staff. They searched through a possible 40 winning systems but could not find a match for the 'lucky Yorkshireman'. Seven days later his secret became apparent, the faulty table was changed from table six to table one, but the shrewd Bradfordian had already marked the offending area and went straight back to his winning streak. When the cylinder had been removed Jagger walked away over two million francs richer, about two million pounds by today's prices! Yes, to coin a phrase he had 'broke the bank'! The casino had learnt its lesson and now the wheels are tested every day before business commences.

Jagger for the rest of his life became bored after giving up his job. He invested heavily in property in the Little Horton area of Bradford, but the story remains all the more incredible after he reputedly employed a team of clerks to record all the numbers showing up on roulette wheels. Jagger spoke no French and was also a Methodist Lay preacher, being a factory worker how could he afford such an elaborate holiday in the first place? A fascinating character who lies buried in a prominent grave at the Bethel Methodist chapel graveyard on the main Halifax road out of Bradford.

Sir Edward Appleton

Many great men and women have been born in humble surroundings in 'old blighty' but one who has gone relatively unnoticed for his achievements is Edward Victor Appleton who was born in 1892 at a back to back house in Maperton Road, Bradford Moor. At a very early age the house was demolished and the family moved to 64 Hanover Square just off Manningham Lane. He attended Hanson secondary school and won a scholarship at Bradford Grammar school, but could not attend due to his family's lack of money (his father was a warehouseman).

On attaining 18 years of age he won the Sir Isaac Holden scholarship to St Johns College Cambridge, graduating with a first class degree in natural sciences. He went on to become Britain's youngest professor and the government chief scientist during the Second World War. His knowledge brought about the advancement of radar and helped to win the Battle of Britain for the allies. He was also involved in perfecting the atomic bomb along with other scientists. Unfortunately science did not attract much attention is his home city, probably because it was surrounded in secrecy therefore Edward never received the recognition he so rightly deserved nationally.

In 1947 he received the Nobel Prize for Physics after he had been knighted in 1941. In 1948 the Pope appointed him to the Pontifical Academy of Science. He died in 1965 after becoming chancellor of Edinburgh University.

Bradford's Great Inventor

Mention the name Edward Spurr to a Bradfordian and they are more than likely so say 'Edward who'? But, this man can be considered Bradford's finest inventor. Edward was born in 1907 at 18 Fagley Terrace and attended Wellington Road Elementary school to be followed by Hanson Grammar school and then a day student at Bradford technical school/college. Education was to follow Edward through his life until he reached 40 years of age. His fellow pupils stated that he excelled at sports, physics and sciences.

Edward entered the world of engineering as a draughtsman with Jowett cars in his home town of Bradford after he had worked his way through the Scott Autocar Company. His fascination for learning took him to other parts of the country completing design work and building up good working relationships that were to stand him in good stead for the rest of his life. One of these working relationships was with a Colonel T.E.Lawrence, formerly Lawrence of Arabia but in the 1930's known as aircraftsman Shaw who helped him design 'Empire Day' a speedboat costing some £8,000 which Edward hoped would break the world class one and half litre record. Life continued and Edward worked with Barnes Wallace on the 'Bouncing Bomb' to destroy German dams in the Second

World War and his technical expertise was used for jet engines on Wellington bombers. Edward continued to travel to all corners of the world and was totally immersed in his work. He designed a car in South Africa and worked for various companies until his retirement in 1977 and died in 1998.

Edward would not have been out of place as a comic book hero, he was so multi-faceted he knew nothing was impossible- a true Bradfordian.

Harry Wardman 'The King of Washington'

Bradford has raised some astute businessmen, but none finer in my opinion than Harry Wardman, a very determined man born in 1873.

Feeling he was getting nowhere fast in his home city he decided to try his luck in America. Queen Victoria's reign was coming to an end when Harry boarded an ocean steamer with a few personal belongings, the clothes he stood up in and his total wealth of 7s6d, or thirty seven and a half pence in decimal currency. He had acquired a variety of skills working in Bradford from messenger boy at Lingards, mill lad, draper and most importantly of all, a joiner which ultimately was to stand him in good stead during his ascendancy. After arriving in the states he took time to familiarise himself with his new home and apprenticed himself to a building contractor. A year went by and sure that he could do the work he decided to go it alone.

He borrowed money and built the Wardman Park Hotel. On completion in 1918 it had 1,000 rooms and other hotels followed and Harry became a very rich man. Further successes followed and with Washington growing at a fast pace population wise Harry secured a deal with the local municipal council housing department and such was his reputation that he became known as the 'King of Washington' and a legend in his home city of Bradford. At one time he is believed to have owned 10% of the housing stock in Washington, second only to the American Government. Confidence in himself abounded but still a cautious and calculated gamble paid off, these qualities enabled him to see his way through the 1929 stock market crash at which point his wealth amassed was said to be six million pounds though real estate bonds.

Married twice he lived life to the full but died young at the age of 65. Unfortunately many young Bradfordians will never have heard of him or his exploits but his incredible story must be told as an example to all young entrepreneurs.

Three Famous Writing Sisters

Without doubt Bradford can claim to be the birthplace of the Bronte sisters although it is not known to the world at large and most people assume Haworth to be their place of birth. Any self-respecting Bradfordian will point to a terraced at a rather deserted Market Street but a plaque marks the spot. Here Reverend Patrick Bronte obtained his first post as clergyman, having married Maria Bramwell in 1812 and then during a seven year period six children cam their way. In 1820 they moved to Haworth and their parsonage, now world famous, facing east and which was subject to strong wind and gales. Mrs Bronte died soon after moving here from cancer and two of the six children passed also. The remaining offspring could only be described as frail, with the exception of Patrick. The three daughters had little more to do than household chores, dined apart from their father. Increasingly they spent more time on the moors which became the inspiration for the books that soon had London talking. The views they had took in the west Ilkley moors to the North Pendle hill. From reading their books you can often imagine the wind whistling round their ears and their feet surrounded by moss and sometimes purple heather. The resultant books have stood the test of time as the hard copies even today are described as works of genius. Wuthering Heights, Jane Eyre and Agnes Gray were classics which followed in quick succession and made a mark on America. The authors were unspoilt by success but also refused to accept failure- Good Bradford qualities I might add!

Many admirers of literature from all over the world now make the pilgrimage to Haworth and its parsonage, the local church and the Black Bull pub where the brother Bramwell spent a lot of his time. Others will traverse the moors to see the tumbled down ruins of a farmhouse 'Top Withens' which Emily used as a scene in Wuthering heights. The very characters used in these fine novels epitomise their landscape and surroundings. The sisters sadly died in a short period of time in the late 1840's at what would be described as a young age. Charlotte had just married and was pregnant when life struck her a cruel blow. Reverend Bronte, the father, outlived his entire family and died in 1861 at the age of 84.

A Man with a Vision

Jonathan Silver shaped the lives of others through his tremendous vitality for life and imagination, innovation and tenacity. Born soon after the Second World War had finished at Clifton Villas, Manningham to Jewish parents Jonathan was soon involved in matters of business whilst still attending school, Bradford Grammar School to be precise. The book did not appeal to him and after leaving school he threw himself into his clothing business which attained a turnover of one million pounds and thirteen retail premises. Yes Jonathan loved a challenge in his life but duly settled down to domesticity in August 1972 with Maggie Jackson but was soon on the outlook for other business ventures. Together with their young family they travelled around the world for eighteen months before returning to buy Dean Clough mills in Halifax. But things did not work out well with his business partner, Ernest Hall. In the mid-eighties Salts Mill came up for sale and Jonathan jumped at the chance to regenerate it. Long hours were spent at the site and an old friendship with David Hockney the Bradford born artist led to his paintings being displayed in a special 1853 gallery on the site. The day after purchasing the site he was offered a profit of one million pounds but he refused. Through sheer hard work he put Saltaire on the tourist trail, and industry was attracted in the form of Pace Technology. Saltaire became a fashionable place and duly became a world heritage site all thanks to the single minded dedication of one man whose vision was achieved before his untimely death in 1997.

Housewives Favourite

Richard Whiteley OBE was the son of Kenneth Whiteley who ran a textile business in Eccleshill which in turn became Studley Wools. Richard was born in 1943 and lived in Baildon. At the age of thirteen he attended Giggleswick public school near Settle and gradually progressed to Cambridge to read English after being taught by Russell Harty. He married in 1971 but the association did not last long and the wife did not feature in his will.

Some years before Richard had joined Yorkshire TV and their Calendar News programme on its formation and he was the first to interview Margaret Thatcher after the Brighton bombing in 1984. He was very knowledgeable on most matters but the quiz show Countdown on Channel 4 made him a TV superstar.

His 200 jackets and alleged 500 ties together with a good working relationship with Carol Vorderman made him the darling of the nation. He died a modest man aged 61, leaving £2.5 million in cash and property. Before his death he was awarded an OBE and appointed one of the Deputy Lord Lieutenants for West Yorkshire. Other awards included being given the honorary title of mayor of Wetwang in East Yorkshire. Such was his fame that more than 250,000 people jammed the switchboard at Yorkshire TV in the days after his death. A huge gathering turned up at York Minster to give him his final send off. He was a man who never forgot his roots despite his immense fame.

The Man Who Turned His Back on Bradford

Frederick Delius was born in Bradford during the year 1862 and is noted to be one of Bradford's greatest sons, although he showed distaste for his home city and left the place as soon as the opportunity arose. His father, Julius was a wool merchant of German- Jewish stock and helped to arrange the subscription concerts at St Georges Hall. Frederick was originally known as Fritz for the first forty years of his life. He attended Bradford Grammar School but did not have the aptitude for the book. After leaving school he worked in his father's business as a travelling rep engaged in textile sales. This position never interested Fritz and he remained an individual with an eye for a musical career. His father sent him to Florida to work on an orange plantation, however after eighteen months he moved to the state of Virginia. Fritz craved for a full time musical career and education and obtained such at Leipzig, Germany before moving to Paris in 1890. Not much is known of this period of his life. He developed a roving eye for women and struck a period of financial hardship when family sponsorship ran out. He was now at the crossroads of his life having completed his musical works and was considering moving back to London. His female companion at the time was a certain Jelka Rosen (who was to become his wife) who had purchased a property at Grez-sur-Loing near Paris. Here he settled to write some of his finest works although he continued to travel in Norway and the USA. Eventually Delius's health began to deteriorate; he began to go blind and lost the use of his limbs.

A fellow Yorkshireman, Eric Fenby heard of his plight and went to live with Delius at Grez and completed his last work by dictation. Delius died in1934 and is buried in Limpfield, Surrey. He had received the ultimate honour from his home city as he was made a Freeman in 1932. Today a plaque stands at the entrance of his birthplace at 6 Claremont in Bradford and a huge skeletal sculpture adorns the front of Bradford's County Court building. There is also a street named after him on the Ravenscliffe estate, plus a bar in the house next door to 6 Claremont, aptly named 'Delius Lived Next Door' but that is all that remains of the musical maestro, who turned his back on his home city to find international fame and a bohemian lifestyle.

The Clown Prince of Soccer

Len Shackleton was born in Bradford on 22nd may 1922. He attended Whetley Hill Junior School and Carlton Grammar School and soon became Bradford's first player to be chosen for the England schools football team. His talent for the round ball was spotted by Arsenal who invited him for trials as an amateur. Little did they realise their mistake at the time as Len later became a cult figure in the North east of England and generally accepted as one of the finest forwards to wear an England shirt. He made his initial work on the game by playing for Bradford Park Avenue at the age of seventeen scoring an amazing 160 goals and dazzling fans with amazing footwork and special silky skills. An English international cap followed in 1945 and a year later he joined Newcastle United playing staff for a paltry sum of £13,000. Soon the magpie fans cottoned onto what a real bargain they had obtained in the transfer market. Newcastle fans held him in awe after an astonishing 13-0 victory on his debut against Newport County (Shackleton scored six goals). Shackleton then moved along the East coast to Sunderland F.C and it wasn't long before the Roker Roar was in evidence. The £20,000 fee was well justified and in all competitions he scored a total of 101 goals for the Black Cats. Amazingly only a few further England caps adorned Lens mantelpiece but this was probably due to his forthright speaking and dislike of football authorities. An injury brought an abrupt end to his career. England's finest only received £17 a week for his endeavours. In terms of transfer fees and wages, how much would he be worth today? The mind boggles! A true hero of the working class people of Bradford and beyond, Even in death he his remembered by his legion of fans. What could the Bradford clubs do with him today?

James Bond and His Life in Bradford

Many younger people born in Bradford will be shocked to learn that the man who liked it 'shaken not stirred' lived a while in Baildon whilst running a textile company in Idle in the late 1960's. Roger Moore had just finished The Saint TV episodes before taking the Bond role in 1973 in Live and Let Die. Moore used to socialise in the Rosse Hotel at the bottom of Moorhead Lane in Saltaire. I personally remember seeing his famous white saloon with 'The Saint' symbol emblazoned on the car not forgetting the halo as he no doubt travelled around the city.

William Fenton

Harry Houdini (real name Enrich Weiss) started life as a magician, but soon moved into escapology. He toured many principle towns in America and Europe before hitting Bradford at the Bradford Palace February 4th to 9th 1901. Houdini became known for escaping from handcuffs and straight jackets and he would frequently ask his audience to challenge him. One gentleman that did was William Fenton, a local locksmith and cycle maker and repairer of Lumb lane, Bradford. The lock William chose to baffle Houdini with was a lock from an old warehouse door which could have been 150 years old. There were apparently only three in existence and measured 12" wide by 8 ½" high and 3 ½" thick. It weighed 7 kilos. William wrote a letter to Houdini challenging him to pick the lock, nothing more, in front of an audience. Houdini declined wishing to examine and possibly take the lock apart. Thirteen years later Houdini once again performed in Bradford and William Fenton re issued his challenge stating that Houdini should pick the lock on the spot without examination. Houdini once again declined stating that he would require

24 hours to study the lock the fact is that Houdini, the world's greatest escapologist had been beaten. The lock was eventually passed down to Fenton's grandson, George E Waddington who placed it on display in his shop window in Carlisle road, Manningham. In the early 1970's the lock was presented to Bradford Industrial Museum on the understanding that the back of the lock must not be removed. The lock remains there this very day!

Chapter 20

Lord Mayors of Bradford

The first Lord Mayor of Bradford was Alderman John Godwin who took up the position on September 16th 1907. Bradford's first Female Lord Mayor was Alderman Kathleen Chambers in 1945, and Bradford was the home of the first Asian Lord Mayor in Councillor Mohammed Ajeeb who took up office in 1985.

1907-1907	John Arthur Godwin
1907-1908	John Edward Fawcett
1909-1910	James Hill
1909-1911	William Laird
1910-1911	Jacob Moser (died in office)
1911-1912	John Batt Moorhouse
1912-1913	Fred Foster
1913-1914	John Arnold
1914-1915	George Henry Robinson
1915-1916	Thomas Haworth
1916-1917	Abram Peel
1917-1918	John Bland (died in office)
1918-1918	Herbert Hustler Tetley
1918-1919	Joseph Hayhurst (died in office)
1919-1919	Walter Barber
1919-1920	William Wade
1920-1921	Anthony Gadie
1921-1922	Thomas Blythe
1922-1923	Thomas Snowden
1923-1924	Herbert Morris Trotter
1924-1925	John Henry Palin
1923-1924	Herbert Morris Trotter
1924-1925	John Henry Palin
1925-1926	Joseph Stringer
1926-1927	Richard Johnson
1927-1928	Michael Conway
1928-1929	Herbert Thornton Pullan

1929-1930	Angus Hardy Rhodes
1930-1931	Alfred Pickles
1931-1932	George Walker
1932-1933	John William Longley
1933-1934	Arthur Walter Brown
1934-1935	Walter Hodgson
1935-1936	Jonas Pearson
1936-1937	George Ripley Carter
1937-1938	Henry Hudson
1938-1939	Thomas Johns Robinson
1939-1940	Meredith Farrar Thompson
1940-1941	William Illingworth
1941-1942	Louis William Squire Smith
1942-1943	James Harrison
1943-1944	Walter Henry Barraclough
1944-1945	Cecil Barnet
1945-1946	Kathleen Chamber
1946-1947	Thomas Illingworth Clough
1947-1949	Fredrick James Cowie
1949-1950	George Thomas Meggison
1950-1951	Alton Ward
1951-1952	Horace Hird
1952-1953	John Shee
1953-1954	Angus Crowther
1954-1955	Henry James White
1955-1955	Herbert William Semper (died in office)
1955-1956	Richard Cornelius Ruth
1956-1957	Horace Robert Walker
1957-1958	David Black
1958-1959	Norbert William Durrant
1959-1960	Ernest England
1960-1961	Edgar Robinson
1961-1962	Benjamin Wilfred Bur
1962-1963	Harold Kershaw Watson
1963-1964	Tom Wood
1964-1965	Weber Marshall Hird
1965-1966	Jack Wilson
1966-1967	Louis Cowgill
1967-1967	Thomas Lee (died in office)

1968-1968	John William Taylor
1968-1969	Arthur Walton
1969-1970	Edward Newby
1970-1971	John Edward Baines Singleton
1971-1972	Herbert Morgan
1972-1973	Audrey Firth
1973-1974	Derek Smith
1974-1974	John Edward Baines Singleton
1974-1975	Thomas Edward Hall
1975-1976	Doris Birdsall
1976-1977	Frank Hillam
1977-1978	Paul Hockney
1978-1979	Arthur Frederick Twigg
1979-1980	John Stuart Senior
1980-1981	Daniel Canon Coughlin
1981-1982	Arnold Lightowler
1982-1983	Joan Lightband
1983-1984	Norma Free
1984-1985	Olive Messer
1985-1986	Mohammed Ajeeb
1986-1987	William Arthur Nunn
1987-1988	Laurence Corral Coughlin
1988-1989	Smith Midgely
1989-1990	George Hogson
1990-1991	Ernest Saville (died in office)
1991-1992	Sydney John Collard
1992-1993	Barry Kenneth Thorne
1993-1994	Robert Sowman
1994-1995	Danny Mangham
1995-1996	Marilyn Beeley
1996-1997	Gordon Mitchell
1997-1998	James Anthony Cairns
1998-1999	Tony Millar
1999-2000	Harry Mason
2000-2001	John Stanley King
2001-2002	Ghazanfer Khaliq
2002-2003	Richard Edward John Wightman
2003-2004	Allan Irving Hilary
2004-2005	Irene Ellison Wood

2005-2006	Valerie Binney
2006-2007	Choudary Rangzeb
2007-2008	Robin Ernest Owens
2008-2009	Howard Middleton
2009-2010	John Godward
2010-2011	Peter Hill
2011-2012	Naveeda Ikram
2012-2013	Dale Smith
2013-2014	Khadim Hussain
2014-2015	Mike Gibbons
2015-2016	Joanne Dodds

Made in the USA
Charleston, SC
27 November 2015